The Lighthouse Keeper's Picnic

Ronda & David Armitage

D0299522

First published in 1993 by Scholastic Ltd
This edition first published in 2008 by Scholastic Children's Books
Euston House, 24 Eversholt Street
London NW1 1DB
a division of Scholastic Ltd
www.scholastic.co.uk
London ~ New York ~ Toronto ~ Sydney ~ Auckland
Mexico City ~ New Delhi ~ Hong Kong

Text copyright © 1993 Ronda Armitage
Illustrations copyright © 1993 David Armitage

ISBN 978 1407 10652 6

All rights reserved
Printed in China

5 7 9 10 8 6

The moral rights of Ronda Armitage and David Armitage have been asserted.

Papers used by Scholastic Children's Books are made from wood grown in sustainable forests.

Mr Grinling was a lighthouse keeper. He lived with his wife Mrs Grinling and their cat Hamish in a little white cottage on the cliffs. When he was a younger man Mr Grinling used to row out to the lighthouse every morning to clean and polish the light. Now he had an assistant called Sam. Some days Mr Grinling was the lighthouse keeper and some days it was Sam.

On his days off there were lots of things Mr Grinling liked to do. He liked playing hide and seek with Hamish, he liked growing geraniums and heliotropes, he liked singing loudly in the village choir but, most of all, he liked eating. Breakfast, lunch and dinner and a few little snacks in between. Eating was what he did best. Sometimes while he ate he would hum a little tune.

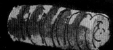

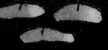

Mrs Grinling worried about the eating. "Mr G, don't you think perhaps you're just a bit too rotund?" she asked. "I don't know how you're going to run races at the village picnic tomorrow."
Mr Grinling gazed at himself in the mirror. "Nonsense, Mrs G," he said as he did up his shirt. But he went outside to practise his running before dinner.

Mr Grinling loved the village picnic. All the villagers came. Big ones and little ones, running and skipping, huffing and puffing. Mrs Grinling always prepared a splendid picnic spread and she always kept it as a surprise.

The picnic day started badly for the Grinlings. They woke up at 9 o'clock instead of 8 o'clock. In the rush Mr Grinling tripped over Hamish. Hamish hid behind the sofa.

They were half way across the bay before they remembered

he was still at home

and half way across again when they remembered

the second lunch basket.

They were very late for the picnic and they forgot to tie up the dinghy.

Everybody was lining up for the egg and spoon race when they arrived. Mr Grinling ran as fast as he was able but he still came last.

He and Joe Jenkins tripped over each other in the three-legged race.

As for the last race he couldn't even fit into the sack, let alone jump.

Mr Grinling was very upset. He stomped off to swim by himself before lunch. He lay on his back with his tummy in the air. Up above a rainbow balloon drifted. Mr Grinling sighed. That would be the life, floating just like a cloud, that's what he'd really like to do. He sang a floating song to himself.

High in the sky
Gently cruising
Wrapped up in cotton wool
Quietly musing
Singing a cloud song

The picnic lunches were magnificent. Mr Grinling wandered about tasting – a little bit here, a little bit there. But he stopped quite still when he saw Mrs Grinling's spread.

Naughty Nibbles

Bumper Bites

Tempting Treats for Tinies

Melon Boat

Limpet Log

Lighthouse Cake

Salad Crab

Great Green Whale Jelly

Cream Whorls

Starfish Sandwiches

Scallop Sausages

Sea Food

"Sea food" she had called it and it was beautiful. Mr Grinling ate a piece of everything. "Delicious and delectable," he announced with his mouth full of green whale jelly. "The best cook here today, Mrs G, possibly the best cook in the whole, wide world."

Once the picnic was eaten everyone was too full to run or jump any more. Most of the villagers packed up their baskets, and went happily home. Mr and Mrs Grinling felt like a rest. They lay in the sun with their heads under their hats and quietly snored.

When they awoke the sun was beginning to fade, the tide was coming in and the dinghy had floated away.
"Well that's that," said Mrs Grinling,
"we'll just have to walk home."
Mr Grinling groaned.

They set off around the rocks. In and out, up and down they went, over and under, rock after rock. Soon the sun had disappeared. The water came closer.

"We must hurry, Mr G," said Mrs Grinling, "the tide is racing in."

But Mr Grinling couldn't hurry. "I can't climb any more," he puffed, "and I certainly can't climb through that hole, I'll get stuck." Mrs Grinling looked at the hole and she looked at Mr Grinling's tummy. "In that case there's nothing for it," she said, "we'll have to stay here till morning."

They found a flat rock and huddled together to keep warm. The moon came up. The water rose. Once a wave splashed their feet a little but it was only once and then the water began to go down.

Sam was surprised to see the lighthouse light still shining next morning. When he saw the dinghy nudging against the jetty below he guessed what had happened. He gazed round the bay. Yes, there they were; jumping up and down and waving.
He set off right away to rescue them.

Mrs Grinling was cross. Mr Grinling didn't think he'd ever seen her quite so cross. "Mr Grinling," she glared, "that was the coldest and most frightening night I have ever had and all because you're so fat!" Mr Grinling sighed, "You're quite right, Mrs G, I am too fat. What shall I do?"

"Well," said Mrs Grinling, "the cakes will have to go AND the chocolates, the crisps and the sweets." Mr Grinling was horrified, all his favourite foods.

He worked very hard
at getting thinner.

He ran up and down
the path from the
little white cottage
to the dinghy.

He cycled like the wind
into the village
and home again.

Some nights he was so tired
that he fell asleep
in his dinner.

But he did miss the little snacks. "Just one chocolate biscuit, Mrs G?" he pleaded.
"No, Mr G," she said firmly, "Not even half of one."

Sam didn't like it when Mr Grinling was unhappy. "I'll get you a little something," he whispered, "Mrs Grinling need never know."

Mr Grinling hid the snacks
very carefully, and he ate
only one thing each day.

But when Mrs Grinling told him to
climb on the scales, he was as
heavy as ever.
"I don't understand," said
Mrs Grinling. "You've been so good,
no chocolates or biscuits."
Mr Grinling gazed at the ceiling.

For the next few days Mrs Grinling watched Mr Grinling very closely. She spied from behind the door when he crept into the living room. "Got you, Mr Grinling!" She pounced as his hand reached into the vase. "You should be ashamed of yourself." Mr Grinling hung his head. "Promise me," said Mrs Grinling, "no more snacks." Mr Grinling sighed, "I promise, Mrs G."

Mr Grinling went on trying to get thinner. One day when he was out cycling with Hamish he saw the rainbow balloon again. It was so close he could hear the gentle roar.

"I'd love to float like that," he thought, "as light as a feather. But then I'm not light." He looked at his round tummy. "I don't suppose I'd even fit in the basket," he said gloomily.

He told Mrs Grinling about the balloon that evening.
"Not for you, Mr G," she said, "they'd never get you off the ground."

Mr Grinling got a surprise in the village next day. He saw a large notice in a house window. He knocked at the door.
"I don't suppose I'd be able to have a ride in your balloon?" he asked.

BALLOON RIDES

The balloon lady gazed at him,
then slowly she walked round him
both ways.
"Of course you can,"
she said,
"and we could probably
take Mrs Grinling as well."
Mr Grinling smiled,
a great beaming smile.

So that's how the Grinlings
went floating one fine afternoon.
Hamish and Sam waved them goodbye.

Up over the lighthouse they went and across the bay.
Past the rock where they'd spent that cold night,
over the sea where the whales dived and played,
over the cliffs where the seagulls nested.
And then the land was below, houses and barns;
cows, sheep and horses.

Mr Grinling smiled at Mrs Grinling. "This is the best thing I have ever done," he said. "It's even better than eating."

High in the sky
Gently cruising
Wrapped up in cotton wool
Quietly musing
Singing a cloud song